SCENE BY SCENE COMPARATIVE WORKBOOKS

The King's Speech
by Tom Hooper

Cultural Context

Literary Genre

General Vision and Viewpoint

Copyright © 2015 by Amy Farrell.

All rights reserved. No part of this publication may be reproduced, distributed or transmitted in any form or by any means, including photocopying, recording, or other electronic or mechanical methods, without the prior written permission of the publisher, except in the case of brief quotations embodied in critical reviews and certain other noncommercial uses permitted by copyright law. For permission requests, write to the publisher, addressed "Attention: Permissions Coordinator," at the address below.

Scene by Scene
11 Millfield, Enniskerry
Wicklow, Ireland.
www.scenebysceneguides.com

orders@scenebyscene.ie

The King's Speech Comparative Workbook HL16 Amy Farrell. —1st ed.
ISBN 978-1-910949-06-1

2016 Higher Level Comparative Workbook

'The King's Speech' by Tom Hooper

The modes at Higher Level for 2016 are:

Cultural Context

This mode refers to the world of the text.

Consider social norms, beliefs, values and attitudes. Think about the roles of men and women and the power structures in this world, etc.

The General Vision and Viewpoint

This mode refers to the author's outlook or view of life and how this viewpoint is represented in the text.

Consider whether the text is bright or dark, optimistic or pessimistic, uplifting or bleak, etc.

Literary Genre

This mode refers to the way the story is told.

Consider the manner and style of narration, characterisation, setting, tension, literary techniques, etc.

About This Workbook

Our workbooks are for the Leaving Certificate Comparative Study.

Each workbook is divided into three coloured sections, one for each comparative mode. This makes it easy to identify each mode and make comparisons and contrasts between texts – simply use matching coloured sections of each of your workbooks to identify similarities and differences.

Each coloured section has two parts to it. The first part focuses on the text itself, and asks text-specific questions within a comparative mode. This helps you get familiar with the text and the aspects of the text that are covered by that mode.

The second part of each section focuses on one of the modes. In this part, you are asked more general, mode-specific questions. You then have to take what you know about the text and apply it to the mode. By doing this you will become very familiar with what each mode involves, and it will help prepare you for writing comparative answers.

Once complete, this workbook will become your set of notes, to revise and study before the exam, and to help you when preparing comparative essays for class.

We hope our workbooks help you conquer the comparative!

Best wishes,

The team at Scene by Scene

scenebysceneguides.com

The King's Speech by Tom Hooper
Cultural Context

THE KING'S SPEECH - CULTURAL CONTEXT

What **time** and **place** is the story set in?

Why is **war** so important in the film?

KNOW THE TEXT

Why is Bertie's stammer so problematic for him?

Why is Wallis Simpson judged to be an unsuitable match for David?

THE KING'S SPEECH - CULTURAL CONTEXT

What forces David to abdicate? What is your reaction to this?

Comment on Lionel Logue's social status.

KNOW THE TEXT

Explain why Bertie finds it difficult to allow himself to be friends with Lionel.

What is significant about Lionel and Bertie being equals when Lionel is treating him?

THE KING'S SPEECH - CULTURAL CONTEXT

What role does Elizabeth, Bertie's wife, play in their marriage? Is she a good wife?

Why does Elizabeth conceal their identities when making appointments? What does this tell you about their world?

KNOW THE TEXT

What strikes you about Bertie's relationship with his children?

What is the religious aspect of being King? What impact does this have on the characters' lives?

THE KING'S SPEECH - CULTURAL CONTEXT

Is life in pre-war London **rigid** and **formal**? Explain your view.

Where do you notice the **class divide** in the film?

KNOW THE TEXT

What is life like for the Royal Family?

THE KING'S SPEECH - CULTURAL CONTEXT

Does Bertie believe in tradition? Explain.

KNOW THE MODE

Is **religion** important in this world? What makes you say this?

THE KING'S SPEECH - CULTURAL CONTEXT

Are **wealth** and **class** important in this world? What view do characters have towards **money**?

KNOW THE MODE

Do the characters in this text hold **traditional beliefs**?

THE KING'S SPEECH - CULTURAL CONTEXT

Is **race** important in this world?

KNOW THE MODE

Are characters **moral** and **upstanding** in this text?

THE KING'S SPEECH - CULTURAL CONTEXT

What do people **value** in this text? (What is important to them? What motivates them to act as they do?)

KNOW THE MODE

What kind of **society** do you see in the text? (How do people treat one another? What do they believe in?)

THE KING'S SPEECH - CULTURAL CONTEXT

Is **family** important in the world of this text?

KNOW THE MODE

How are **women** viewed and treated in this story?

THE KING'S SPEECH - CULTURAL CONTEXT

How are **children** viewed and treated in this story?

KNOW THE MODE

Is **friendship/love** important in this world or are characters self-centred and self-serving? (Is it a warm/loving place or a cold/unloving place?)

THE KING'S SPEECH - CULTURAL CONTEXT

Is there **conflict** or **violence** in this world? Where do you see it?

KNOW THE MODE

Is this a **secure** or **dangerous** world?

KNOW THE MODE

Is this a **secure** or **dangerous** world?

THE KING'S SPEECH - CULTURAL CONTEXT

In this world, do characters **conform** or make their own choices **freely?**

KNOW THE MODE

Would you like to live in the world of the text? Use examples to support the points you make.

THE KING'S SPEECH - CULTURAL CONTEXT

Identify the **key moments** in the film that illustrate the Cultural Context of the text.

KNOW THE MODE

THE KING'S SPEECH - CULTURAL CONTEXT

What similarities do you notice in the Cultural Context of this text and your other comparative texts?

KNOW THE MODE

THE KING'S SPEECH - CULTURAL CONTEXT

What **differences** do you notice in the Cultural Context of this text and your other comparative texts?

KNOW THE MODE

KNOW THE MODE

The King's Speech by Tom Hooper
Literary Genre

KNOW THE TEXT

How is the story told? (Consider the film format)

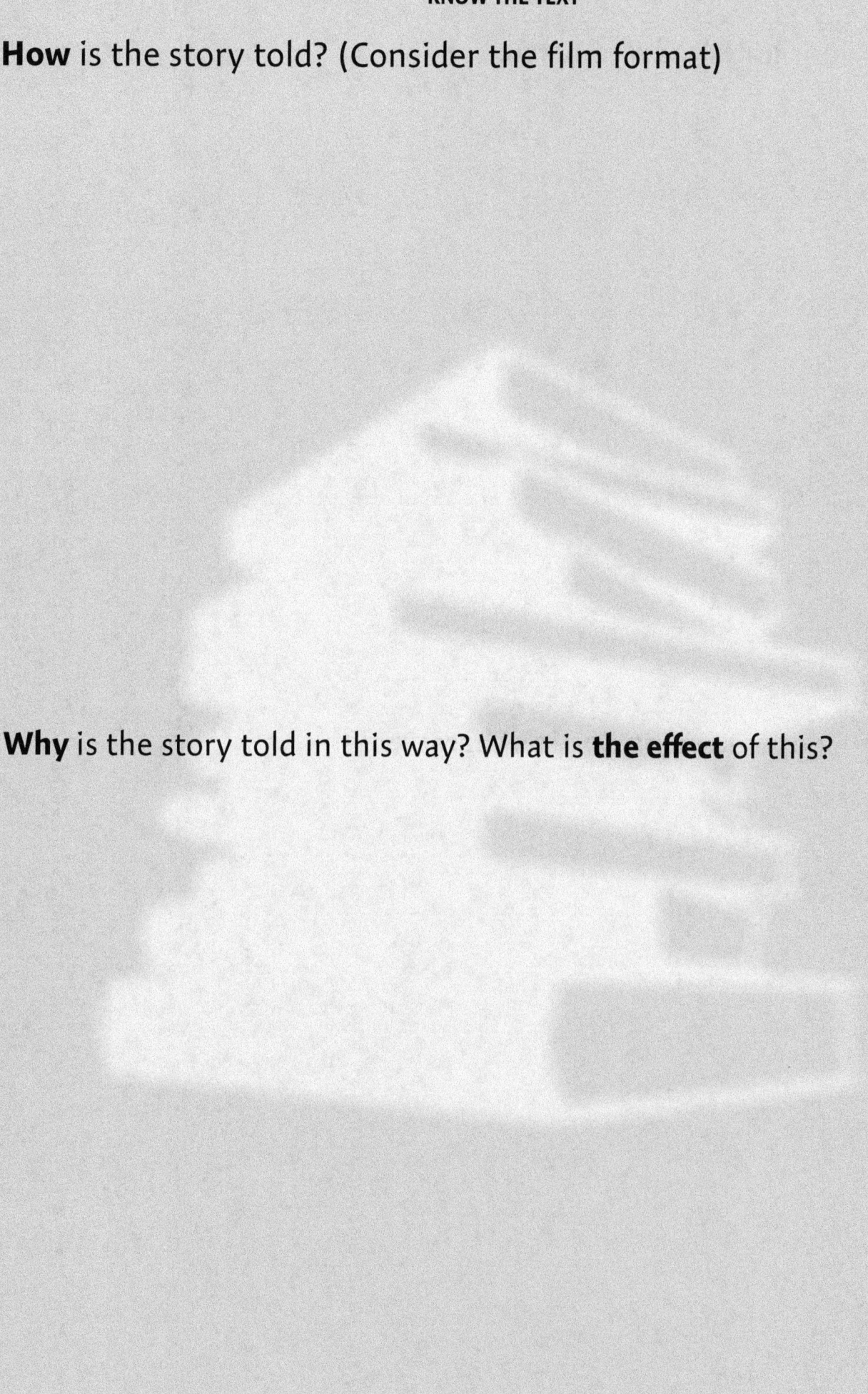

Why is the story told in this way? What is **the effect** of this?

THE KING'S SPEECH - LITERARY GENRE

What was your **initial view** of **Bertie**?

How does Hooper **develop Bertie's character**?

KNOW THE TEXT

What was your **initial view** of **Lionel**?

How does Hooper **develop Lionel's character**?

THE KING'S SPEECH - LITERARY GENRE

What is your opinion of Elizabeth, Bertie's wife?

Which characters do you like? What makes them appealing?

KNOW THE TEXT

Which characters do you dislike? What makes them unappealing?

Where do we see **humour** in the film? What is the effect of this?

What **music** is used in the soundtrack? How does this contribute to the movie?

Is this a film about duty, friendship, bravery or something else?

KNOW THE TEXT

What major themes can you identify?

Comment on the **costumes** in the film. How do they help to tell the story?

THE KING'S SPEECH - LITERARY GENRE

How does the historical aspect contribute to the storytelling here?

Does the fact that many characters are royalty add to the story in any way?

KNOW THE TEXT

In its review, The New York Post called this film an "immense crowd-pleaser." Do you agree with this comment?

THE KING'S SPEECH - LITERARY GENRE

KNOW THE MODE

Did **you** enjoy the **storyline** of the text? (Was it exciting/compelling/tense/emotional? Why/why not?)

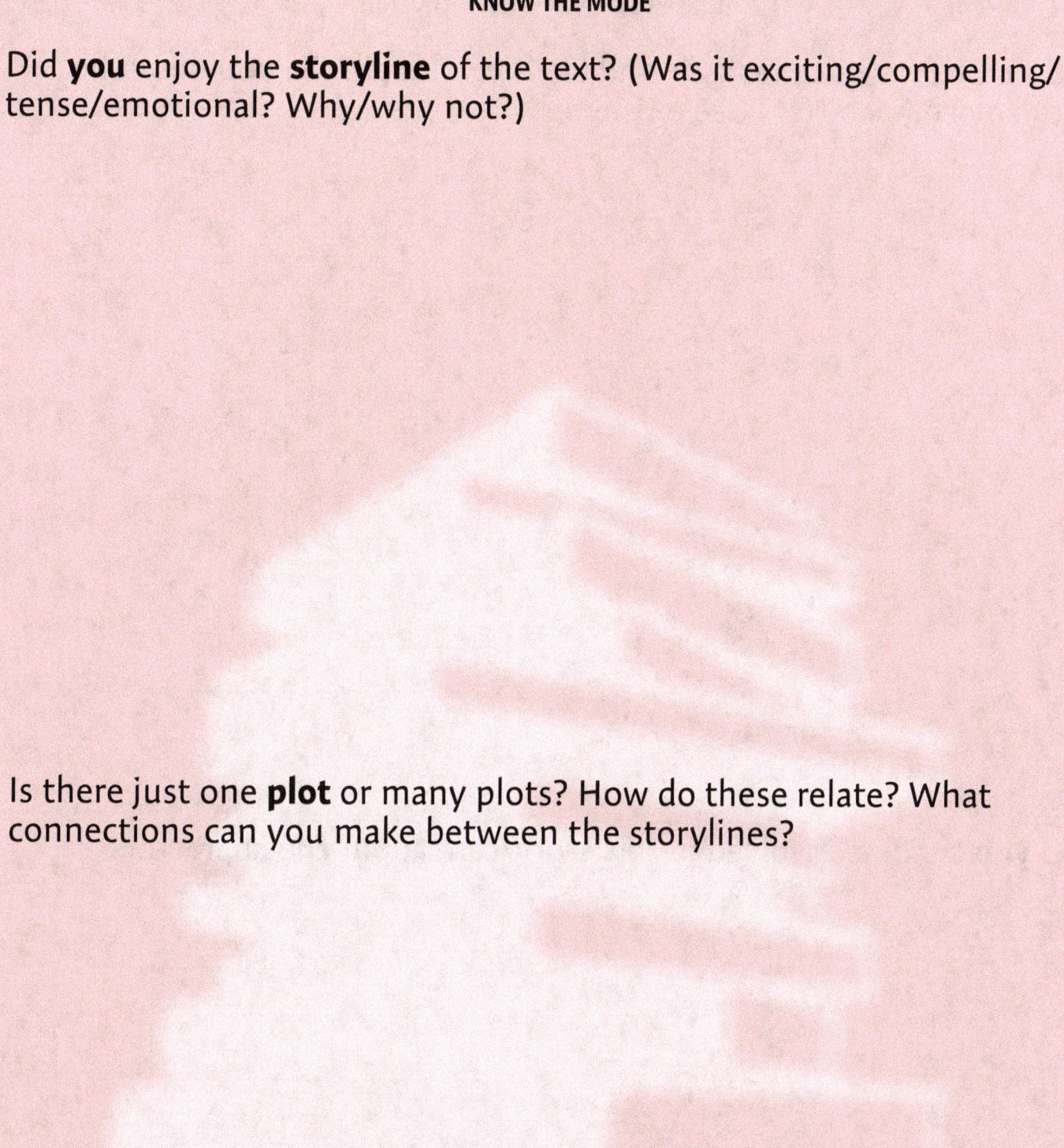

Is there just one **plot** or many plots? How do these relate? What connections can you make between the storylines?

Are **characters** vivid, realistic and well-developed? Do **you** empathise with any character(s)? Use examples.

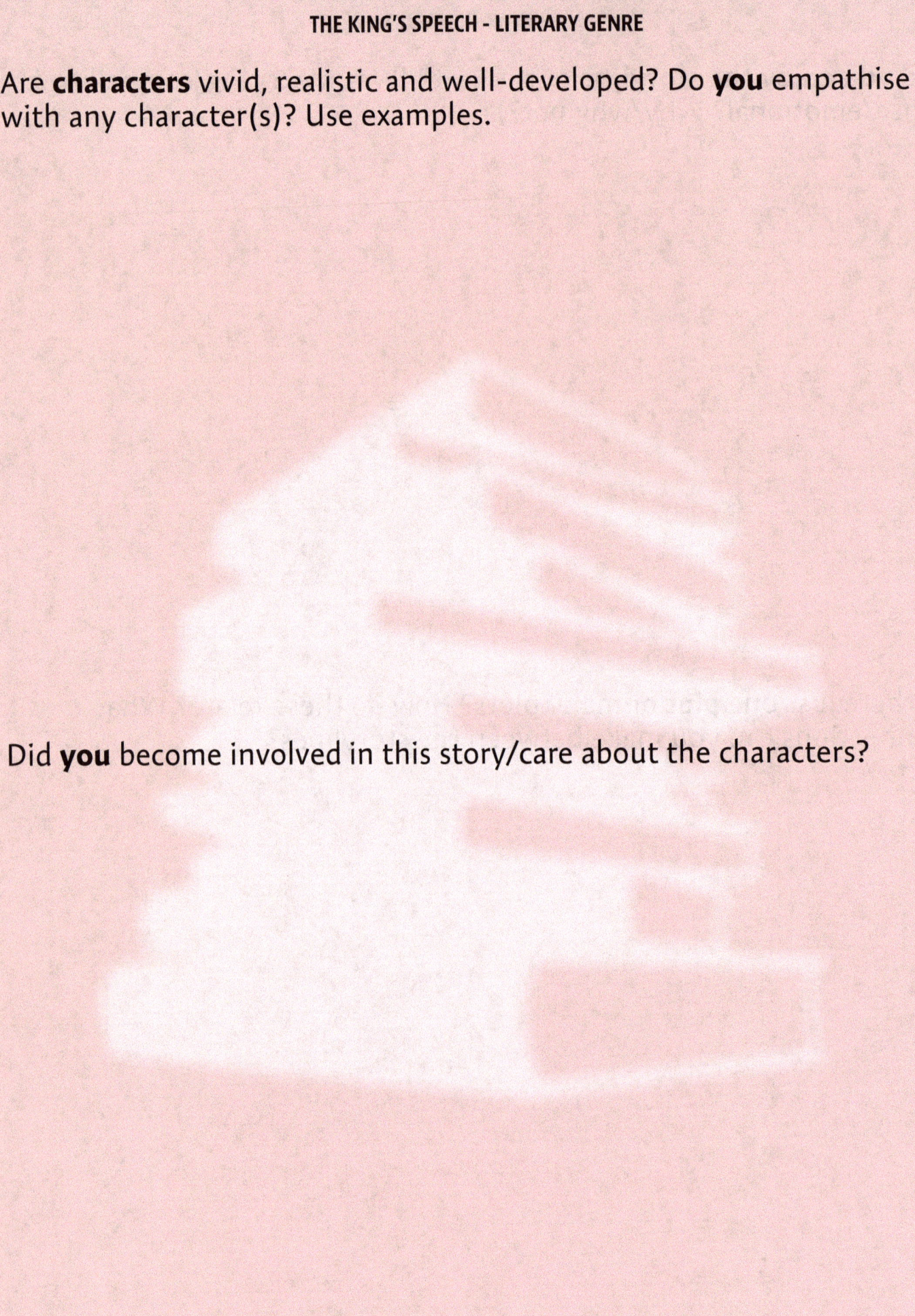

Did **you** become involved in this story/care about the characters?

KNOW THE MODE

Who was your **favourite character**? What aspects of this character did you enjoy?

Who was your **least favourite character**? What aspects of this character did you dislike?

KNOW THE MODE

Is the story humorous or tragic, romantic or realistic? Explain.

To what **genre** does it belong? Is it Romance, Thriller, Social Realism, Saga, Historical, Fantasy, Science-fiction, Satire, etc.?

THE KING'S SPEECH - LITERARY GENRE

How does the director create **tension**, **suspense, high emotion** and **excitement** in the text? What techniques does he use to good advantage?

KNOW THE MODE

Consider the director's use of **tension** and **resolution** in the film. What are the major **tensions/problems/conflicts** in the text? Are they **resolved** or not?

How does the director make points to his audience/force us to think/ introduce themes?

Did the director make use of any striking patterns of **imagery** or **symbols** to add to the story?

KNOW THE MODE

What is the **climax** (high point) of the story? How did you respond to it?

THE KING'S SPEECH - LITERARY GENRE

Comment on the **language** of the film.

KNOW THE MODE

Comment on the **setting** of the film.

THE KING'S SPEECH - LITERARY GENRE

Was anything about this film **moving** or **emotional**? How did this emotion add to the story?

KNOW THE MODE

Did you enjoy the **ending**? What was satisfying/unsatisfying about it?

THE KING'S SPEECH - LITERARY GENRE

The experiences of encountering a play (performed), reading a novel and viewing a film are very different. What aspects of the **film form** worked well in this story, in your opinion? Was **this way** of telling the story **successful** and **enjoyable**? What did **you like** about the **way this story was told**? Mention aspects of literary technique that **you** found appealing and enjoyable. (Make use of personal response – your reaction to key moments)

KNOW THE MODE

KNOW THE MODE

THE KING'S SPEECH - LITERARY GENRE

Identify **key moments** in the film that illustrate Literary Genre (the way the story is told). Clearly define literary techniques in your analysis.

KNOW THE MODE

THE KING'S SPEECH - LITERARY GENRE

What **similarities** do you notice in the Literary Genre of this film and your other comparative texts?

KNOW THE MODE

KNOW THE MODE

THE KING'S SPEECH - LITERARY GENRE

What **differences** do you notice in the Literary Genre of this film and your other comparative texts?

KNOW THE MODE

KNOW THE MODE

THE KING'S SPEECH - LITERARY GENRE

The King's Speech by Tom Hooper
General Vision and Viewpoint

THE KING'S SPEECH - GENERAL VISION AND VIEWPOINT

Do Bertie and Elizabeth love and support one another?

Is Bertie under a lot of pressure in this film?

KNOW THE TEXT

How do you feel watching Bertie's early attempts at public speaking?

Does privilege and celebrity bring the Royal Family happiness? What does this tell us about life?

THE KING'S SPEECH - GENERAL VISION AND VIEWPOINT

What does his friendship with Lionel add to Bertie's life?

How does war looming in the background add to the atmosphere?

KNOW THE TEXT

David abdicates in order to marry for love. What comment does his abdication make on the characters' lives?

Are characters in this film happy and content or dissatisfied with life? Explain.

Why do Bertie and Lionel argue in Westminster Cathedral? How do you feel watching this scene?

Were you hopeful about the film's ending, or did you dread the outcome?

KNOW THE TEXT

How do you feel when Bertie successfully delivers his radio address at the end?

Did you ever truly fear that Bertie would fail? Explain your answer.

THE KING'S SPEECH - GENERAL VISION AND VIEWPOINT

How does the closing section make you feel?

Did you anticipate a happy ending?

KNOW THE TEXT

Is Bertie's future promising?

What is Tom Hooper telling us about life in this story?

Is his outlook positive or negative, in your view?

The Wall Street Journal described this as, "a film that makes your spirit soar." Is this an accurate statement?

KNOW THE TEXT

THE KING'S SPEECH - GENERAL VISION AND VIEWPOINT

Identify bright/hopeful/optimistic moments, or aspects of the film.

KNOW THE MODE

Identify dark/hopeless/pessimistic moments, or aspects of the film.

THE KING'S SPEECH - GENERAL VISION AND VIEWPOINT

Is this text **optimistic** or **pessimistic**? Explain.

KNOW THE MODE

What **aspects of life** does the director concentrate on? Why does he do this?

THE KING'S SPEECH - GENERAL VISION AND VIEWPOINT

What **comments** do characters make on their **society** and the problems they're facing?

KNOW THE MODE

Are characters happy or unhappy?

THE KING'S SPEECH - GENERAL VISION AND VIEWPOINT

What makes characters in this story happy and fulfilled?

KNOW THE MODE

What makes characters in this story unhappy and unfulfilled?

THE KING'S SPEECH - GENERAL VISION AND VIEWPOINT

Are **relationships** destructive or nurturing?

What do they reveal about life, as we see characters supported/thwarted in their efforts to grow/mature?

KNOW THE MODE

Are **imagery** and **language** bright or dark in the text? (Tone of the text)

THE KING'S SPEECH - GENERAL VISION AND VIEWPOINT

What is the **mood** of this text?

KNOW THE MODE

Did you notice the use of symbolism to add to mood or atmosphere anywhere in the text?

THE KING'S SPEECH - GENERAL VISION AND VIEWPOINT

What does this story teach us about life?

KNOW THE MODE

What **view of life** is offered in the text?

THE KING'S SPEECH - GENERAL VISION AND VIEWPOINT

How do you **feel** as you watch this film?

KNOW THE MODE

How do you **feel** at the **end**?

THE KING'S SPEECH - GENERAL VISION AND VIEWPOINT

Are questions raised by the text resolved by the end? Are they resolved happily or unhappily?

KNOW THE MODE

Are *you* **hopeful** or **despairing** regarding the prospects for human **happiness** in this story?

On a scale of one to ten (with one being "most optimistic" and ten being "most pessimistic"), where would you place this text? Explain your choice.

THE KING'S SPEECH - GENERAL VISION AND VIEWPOINT

Identify the **key moments** in the film that illustrate the General Vision and Viewpoint of the text.

KNOW THE MODE

THE KING'S SPEECH - GENERAL VISION AND VIEWPOINT

What **similarities** do you notice in the General Vision and Viewpoint of this text and your other comparative texts?

KNOW THE MODE

THE KING'S SPEECH - GENERAL VISION AND VIEWPOINT

What **differences** do you notice in the General Vision and Viewpoint of this text and your other comparative texts?

KNOW THE MODE

www.ingramcontent.com/pod-product-compliance
Lightning Source LLC
Chambersburg PA
CBHW050714090526
44587CB00019B/3377